ZOOMABABY

and the Search for the Lost Dummy

written by Michael Rosen

illustrated by Caroline Holden

5

And just like that, Zoomababy flapped his arms, and flew out through the window and up into the air.

Zoomababy looked down on the town. There
was Story Street School. He could see the children
playing kiss chase in the playground.

There was an ambulance arriving at the hospital.

Old Crackers the Crow was sitting on White Flag Castle.

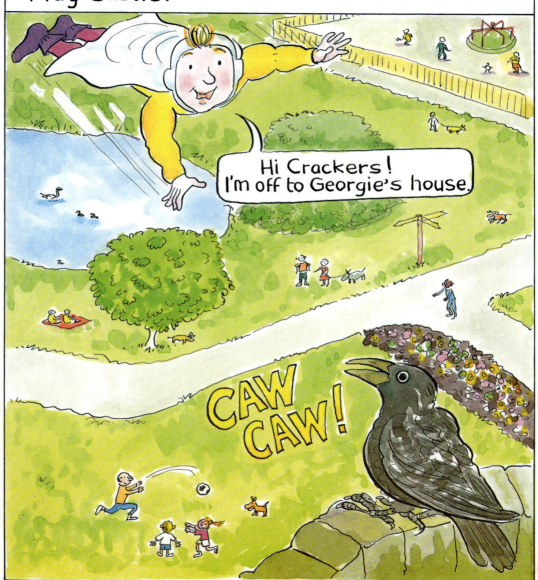

Zoomababy was heading for the flats near the fire station — top floor. Over the railway...

and in through the window of Georgie's flat.

Oh dear! Georgie was sitting in his playpen, sobbing.
He was crying . . . and crying . . . and crying.

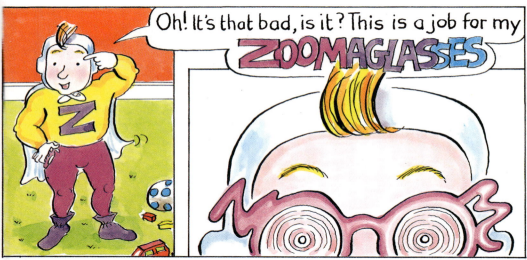

No, it's not there.

Is it in Georgie's dad's shoe?

No, it's not there.

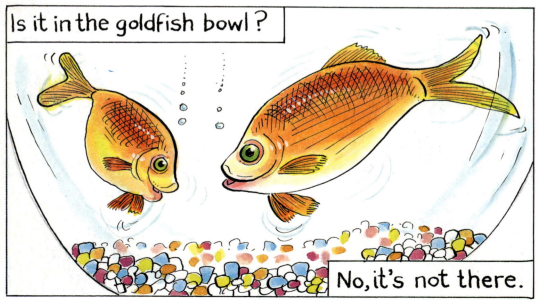

Is it in the goldfish bowl?

No, it's not there.

He took one more look around the room.

The Zoomaglasses zoomed in on Harry Hippo.

He flew over, whipped it out of Harry's ear, and handed it over to Georgie.

SWOOP!

Georgie was overjoyed.

17

Meanwhile, back in Pip's kitchen, Mum was just about to turn around.

The high chair was empty.

Would she turn around...

...before Zoomababy had come back?

19

Zoomababy zoomed up and out of the window...

... and over Story Street.

Over the hospital, over the school...

and in through the kitchen window.

Mum was turning round. Would she see the empty chair?

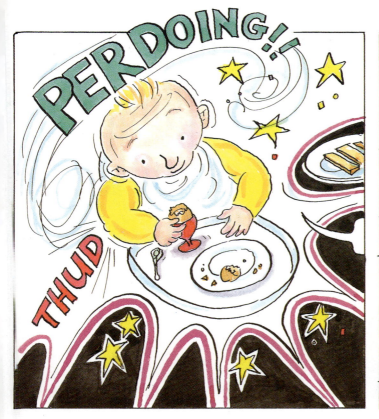

23

All OK Georgie?

Ok thanks Zoomababy.

FLUP

Has the dummy still got a nice taste?

I'm not sucking it, I needed it to stop my playpen squeaking.

Oh! Funny old Georgie!